UNEXPLAINABLE HAPPENINGS

CHILLING TRUE STORIES

Compiled and edited by
Autumn Barnes

&

Tom Lyons

UNEXPLAINABLE HAPPENINGS:
CHILLING TRUE STORIES

Copyright © 2023 Autumn Barnes &
Tom Lyons

All rights reserved. No part of this may
be reproduced without the author's prior
consent, except for brief quotes used in
reviews.

All information and opinions expressed
in *Unexplainable Happenings: Chilling
True Stories* are based upon the
personal perspectives and experiences of
those generous enough to submit them.
The authors do not purport that the
information presented in this book is
based on accurate, current, or valid
scientific knowledge.

Acknowledgments

It's certainly no easy task for people to discuss their encounters with cryptids. I want to thank the many good people who took the time and energy to put their experiences into writing.

To respect those involved, a few of the following names were altered or replaced with "anonymous."

Would you like to see your report in an issue of *Unexplainable Happenings?*

If so, all you have to do is type up a summary of your experience and email it to Tom Lyons at:

Living.Among.Bigfoot@gmail.com

Special Offer

If you submit a report and it is accepted, you will receive an exclusive paperback copy signed by Tom shortly after the book is released. If you'd like to participate in that offer, be sure to include your mailing address in the email.

Contents

Report #1 1

Report #2 7

Report #3 13

Report #4 20

Report #5 26

Report #6 42

Report #7 52

Report #8 63

Report #9 75

Report #10 81

Report #11 88

Report #12 94

Report #13 104

Conclusion.. 111

Editor's Note 113

Mailing List Sign-Up Form 115

Social Media.. 117

About the Author 119

UNEXPLAINABLE HAPPENINGS: CHILLING TRUE STORIES

Report #1

Since the day I was born, the city has been all I've ever known. The constant noise, bright lights, and strangers in passing were my usual, and I never strayed far from my metropolitan area until I was thirty. Miami, to be exact, was my home.

It was my friend's twenty-fifth birthday when the encounter took place. She decided to hit a local club with a group of girlfriends, and though my head was pounding and drinking was far from desirable to me at the time, I tagged along. The drinks weren't doing the job, either. Have you ever experienced a time when no amount of alcohol could get you drunk? It was one of those nights. Some say the cause of random heavyweight experiences stems from a sober mindset. Anyway, the drinks weren't hitting, and around midnight my head started to throb worse than before. Because of all this, I decided to leave early. Luckily, my apartment was only three blocks away from the club.

UNEXPLAINABLE HAPPENINGS: CHILLING TRUE STORIES

People crowded the entire first block on my journey home; more bodies flooded the sidewalks than I'd ever seen, making me wonder if there was an event or holiday that I was unaware of. By the time I reached the second block, nobody was around. The area I lived in was never that silent. Strangers were constantly pacing around, cars were always on the road, and loud music echoed from nearby clubs on any given night. The silence made me nervous. If anything were to happen to me, there'd be no witnesses, and that thought started to pick at me.

Before reaching the third block, I stopped under a street light and lit a cigarette. As I did this, the light above me started to flicker. I ignored it and continued to smoke my cigarette where I stood. Then there was a loud popping noise followed by instant darkness. The bulb blew. Thinking nothing of it, I continued to walk home. Not even a minute passed before I heard another popping sound behind me. Another street light went out.

Weirded out but not necessarily scared, I picked up my pace. The faster I walked, the quicker the lights went out. One by one, every spotlight I'd walk into called for yet another blown lightbulb. It was like I had powers that allowed me to absorb every ray of light in my path, leaving nothing but darkness. After five consecutive streetlights went out as I passed them, fear struck me like lightning. I started to sprint as fast as possible, repeatedly running towards the light just for it to go away.

When I opened the stairway door to my apartment and took my first steps inside, I thought I'd be safe from whatever was happening outside, but I was wrong. Soon as I reached the second story of my building, exactly halfway to my unit, every light in the stairway started to strobe before sharply turning off. I was submerged in complete darkness, unable to see the stairs before me. Despite being visionless, I ran up the stairs, leaping over the steps frantically until I reached my door. There weren't any sounds or sightings to insinuate somebody followed me. It was a matter of every light I passed abruptly turning off.

Everything went back to normal once I was locked inside my apartment. All the lights functioned normally, not flickering or turning off by themselves. I did burn sage regularly in my home, not for spiritual purposes, but for the scent. Perhaps the constant burning of sage created a shield that blocked unwanted energy from coming into my home. I have never experienced anything relatively like that since, but it does make me wonder; what the fuck was that? And why was it happening to me?

UNEXPLAINABLE HAPPENINGS: CHILLING TRUE STORIES

Report #2

For women, the fear of walking alone at night is universal. The list of potentially dreadful outcomes is never-ending; that's why many of us carry pepper spray, a knife, or adopt a dog for protection. I bought an emotional support dog for my peace of mind as a woman who walks home from work every night. I've never faced danger while trekking alone, but I'm humbled enough to acknowledge that I can be vulnerable.

I work the late shift and close the office at night. So, like every other night, I locked up and started heading home with my dog, Jax, by my side. The walk home takes longer with him since it's his last opportunity to go 'potty' before bed. Our route ventures through downtown's main street, then down a well-lit alleyway for an additional mile to get to my apartment.

While walking down the familiar alleyway, the marking point that home is near, Jax started aggressively barking in the direction we were heading. We came to a halt as

I tried to see what he was warning me about, but I didn't see anyone or anything. It was only us. I ensured Jax everything was all right and commanded him to stop barking. A brief moment passed before Jax started to bark again, only he pointed his body behind us as if someone were following us. I observed our surroundings very closely, wondering if there was something I wasn't picking up on. Jax was very well-trained. He wouldn't bark if there weren't a good reason to.

After anxiously noting our surroundings from all angles, I again concluded that there was no danger and ordered Jax to be quiet. Less than one minute later, he started barking behind us again, struggling to turn us around and face whatever followed. This time I ignored him and tugged on his leash to keep moving forward with me, not bothering to look back. That's what I regret, not looking back. I pulled and tugged until, eventually, Jax let out a very loud and painful yelp. I instantly stopped and turned my attention toward Jax, panicking at the thought that I had hurt him, but it wasn't me.

A gruesome cut ran down the right side of his torso, his flesh exposed and blood spilling onto the pavement. I ripped off my shirt without forethought, tied it tightly around his ribcage to slow the blood spill, then threw him over my shoulder and ran to my car. We were fortunate to be about a quarter mile from home and to have my car keys on me because time was not on our side. The vet told us that we would've lost Jax if we'd made it to the hospital five minutes later than we did. It was a miracle that he survived. They also said it was impossible to know what had cut him. There weren't bacteria in his wound, metal or glass shards, nothing. They asked, jokingly, "was he cut by the air?"

"It sure seems like it," I replied.

In all seriousness, the incident with Jax felt like a scene from the 'Paranormal Activity' movies. His wound made it evident that danger was near all along; I couldn't see it.

Since then, I've only driven to work and back, not willing to risk my fur baby or myself getting hurt again.

UNEXPLAINABLE HAPPENINGS: CHILLING TRUE STORIES

Report #3

Greetings from Indiana. My name is Jonny, and I'm a fifth-generation farmer from Mansfield. My life is relatively simple, though a farmer's life has its challenges. I wake up before sunrise every day and perform hard labor until sundown, with the occasional help from my son. He recently turned ten years old and is very involved in

UNEXPLAINABLE HAPPENINGS: CHILLING TRUE STORIES

school and sports, so he only spends time around the farm on weekends.

One typical weekday evening, my son, Junior, had an away soccer game that his mother took him to while I stayed home and tended to our livelihood. Once completing the day's work, I decided to enjoy a couple of drinks in the barn before heading inside. I don't have a drinking problem, but I have a whiskey bar set up below my hay loft for when I feel like rewarding myself for a hard day's work. It was one of those days; the late August sun was beating on me like no tomorrow, and I was exhausted and sore once it set below the mountain.

After finishing my first glass, I heard a child's giggle echo above me in the loft. It was so vivid that I walked across the barn to get a good look and see if my son was sneaking up on me. No one was up there, so I checked my watch and noted that they wouldn't be home for another hour. I must've been hearing things, I thought. I walked back to the whiskey bar, poured another drink, and heard it again. Only this time, it was undoubtedly my son's voice, and in between the laughter, he shouted, "dad!"

"You guys are home already?" I asked, walking up the staircase to the loft. He didn't respond, and once I got up there, my son was gone. "All right, Junior, I'm not in the mood to play Hide and Seek," I called out. Though I kept it casual, I was astounded by the possibility of him not being upstairs. The only way in and out of the loft is the stairway. He didn't go down them to leave, yet he wasn't in the loft where I heard him. Starting to get a little spooked, I turned to walk back down the stairs, and that's when I saw my son run into the tool stall.

"How'd you get down there!" I shouted, and his uncontrollable laughter echoed throughout the building. I rushed to the stall to ask him how we moved across the barn like that, but to my bewilderment, he wasn't there. "I'm done playing with you, Junior!" I said, now irritated. "Stop running around the barn!"

"Honey?" my wife stood in the doorway, puzzling at me. "Who's running around the barn?"

"Junior. He keeps running around and hiding. And he's not listening to me either,"

"No, Junior is inside waiting for us at the dinner table. I made lasagna before the game, have to heat it real quick," she said hesitantly. "Jonny, are you okay?" she asked with sincere concern. My heart dropped to my stomach. There wasn't just a kid running around; it was our kid. I saw him with my own eyes. It didn't make any sense.

"So, there's no chance in hell that Junior could've been here. Is that what you're telling me?" I asked.

UNEXPLAINABLE HAPPENINGS: CHILLING TRUE STORIES

"We just got home. Are you sure you're okay?"

"I'm fine," I grunted, not bothering to explain further. I looked around the barn before heading out with my wife. There was no sign of him anywhere. It was as if I was indeed losing my mind.

When we got to the house, I saw Junior sitting at the dinner table, where my wife said he was, waiting for us. I asked him if he was in the barn just now, and he said no, he'd been inside the house since getting home. So, I let it go without additional questioning. But it still crosses my mind often— why was I seeing my son if he wasn't there, and what was the

UNEXPLAINABLE HAPPENINGS: CHILLING TRUE STORIES

cause of such a thing? The whole occurrence creeps me out.

UNEXPLAINABLE HAPPENINGS: CHILLING TRUE STORIES

Report #4

A few years ago, I went camping with my brother and his friends in the San Diego mountains. They had found an uninhabited plot of land alongside an idle road without any indication of private property and turned it into their secret place. My brother had gone camping there a few times and was eager to show me, so I made the trip down from where I lived in Santa Cruz for a weekend.

His friends were sweet but had strong personalities. I was the only woman there, which was fine with me, but once the joint was getting passed in rotation and I was stoned, my social anxiety started to hit me like a train. Everyone was laughing and being loud around the fire while I sat on a blanket, alone, staring off and stuck in my head. My brother noticed this and approached me subtly, asking if I wanted to go on a walk with him. I nodded in agreement and stood up, following him down a trail that led to a large clearing.

"Look at the stars," he told me, "They're so beautiful tonight. You can see everything."

"Yeah, they're stunning. I needed a camping trip so badly. I just shouldn't have smoked while being in a bad headspace," I said. My brother told me it was okay, that he loved me, and that good people surrounded us. As he consoled me, something stood out from my peripheral view, absorbing more of the moon's light than the dark trees and bushes surrounding it.

I turned my attention down from the sky and saw what looked exactly like a goat demon standing four feet in front of me. It was an abnormally large goat head with long, curved horns and black eyes. It was staring right at me.

"Do you see that?" I calmly asked my brother, keeping my eyes directed at the goat head. I sensed him redirect his attention toward it, then he replied:

"Uh, that goat?" with a hesitant and shaky voice. That confirmed it; I wasn't just high and freaking out. My brother, much soberer and mentally more capable than me at the time, was seeing the same thing I was.

"Uh, yeah..." I said, and we nervously laughed together before simultaneously turning our backs to it and speed-walking to the fire, trying our best not to panic. As we entered the fire's glow and were surrounded by

his friends again, my brother
announced to the group:

"Don't go in that direction;
there's a fucking goat demon." He
laughed nervously, trying to make
light out of it.

"A what?" a friend laughed,
thinking we were just high and
paranoid.

"No, we just saw a giant fucking
goat head with horns staring at us in
the dark!" I chimed in, and my brother
confirmed what I was saying.
Everyone picked at us, saying we
smoked too much, but we both knew
what we saw. Besides, my brother
wasn't even that stoned. He's a
heavyweight and seemed completely

clearheaded compared to everyone else.

He continues to go there with his friends and now refers to that spot as 'the goat place.' I, however, have not returned. He claims he hasn't seen it since and isn't too concerned about it, but it was creepy enough for me! I'd be content never returning to that mountain.

UNEXPLAINABLE HAPPENINGS: CHILLING TRUE STORIES

Report #5

When I was in high school, my group of friends and I were the classic misfits; shitty home lives, constantly skipping class, and always on a new adventure pursuing new highs. Sneaking out at night was frequent; most nights, each other was all we had. We'd climb up the abandoned local search tower with a case of beers, go to the ski resort

UNEXPLAINABLE HAPPENINGS: CHILLING TRUE STORIES

during its after-hours and sled, or drive around to be anywhere but home.

One random weekday, our friend Camille asked us during lunch if we'd ever been to the abandoned fairground a couple of towns over. After saying we hadn't, she told us she would take us later that night. Ecstatic, we all planned to be outside our homes and ready for her to pick us up around midnight. After lunch, we all split up, and I couldn't hold in my excitement for this new exploration.

A quarter past twelve, I saw Camille's headlights pull up to the end of my driveway. I climbed onto the roof outside my bedroom window, threw a thick comforter down on the grass, and jumped onto it—my most common exit plan. I then picked up the blanket and put it in the trunk of Camille's car in case we wanted it for sitting later. Everyone else was already in her vehicle, so I had to sit atop my friend Tony's lap for the car ride.

Everyone was instantly hyped for the night's journey when we pulled into the fairground parking lot. Weeds have grown tall between every flaw in the pavement, and in the distance, we could see a Ferris Wheel with ivy covering nearly every inch of its structure. We hopped out, a few of us holding flashlights, and happily walked into the fairgrounds. We first encountered a game stand, where you shoot at the wooden ducks and potentially win a stuffed animal. Everything was still intact except for the thick layer of dust coating it.

Two friends jumped behind the counter and grabbed large stuffed animals, laughing about how incredible this experience was. After that, we slowly split off and ventured independently, finding fascination in different things. Tony and I went to the Ferris Wheel and sat on one of the bottom seats.

"Do you think it'll break with us on it?" he asked.

"No, this is thick metal; it won't break."

UNEXPLAINABLE HAPPENINGS: CHILLING TRUE STORIES

"Yeah, but look how old it is. Did Camille ever mention when this place shut down? It had to have been fifty years ago. It's so sad looking."

"It does look like we're in an apocalypse movie. There's something beautiful about it, though. It's like time traveling. The whole place is frozen in time," as I finished my sentence, the unexplainable happened. Every light on the Ferris Wheel lit up beneath the ivy, and a loud buzzing sound came from it. Our seat started to shake as if it were glitching. It tried to spin, but the densely layered vines kept it from rotating. Tony and I jumped off it and stared at the ride in astonishment.

UNEXPLAINABLE HAPPENINGS: CHILLING TRUE STORIES

"Holy shit!" he yelled. "There's no way that just turned on!" We stared at it with our jaws dropped to the floor. How could that be possible? We shouted for our friends to come and observe, but no one was around to watch the magic happen, so we ran to where we last saw the others. On our way back to the starting point, Tony and I passed our friend Marcus. He was sitting on one of the game booth chairs, talking to himself. We stopped to listen. Marcus was seemingly conversing with someone, but nobody else was nearby. He was talking to thin air as if somebody had sat beside him.

"Don't worry; you're not stuck here. Get a ride home with my friends and me. I know they won't mind," he said, facing the chair beside him. Chills ran down my spine as soon as I heard him say, *don't worry, you're not stuck here.* He was interacting with something we couldn't see or hear.

"Marcus?" I asked, frightened.

"Oh, hey, guys. This is Maryanne," he said, happily gesturing his hand beside him. "She got stuck here somehow and needs a ride home tonight."

"Marcus, nobody is there," Tony said defensively.

"What are you talking about?" he laughed, then turned his head back towards 'Maryanne,' only to no longer see her. "Wait, where'd she go?" he asked, looking at us in shock. We didn't respond, yet the look on our faces must've said it all. "She was never there?" he quivered.

"No, she wasn't, and we should probably leave," I said.

"Wait, we have to show him the Ferris Wheel," Tony turned to Marcus, "dude, the Ferris Wheel just turned on by itself while we were sitting on it!" Tony said in excitement, apparently unbothered by everything going on around us.

"What the fuck?" Marcus whispered. "Where's everyone else?"

"No idea; we were just looking for you guys," I told him. Marcus rose to his feet and started to walk away.

"Well, let's find them right now." We walked around the grounds calling everyone's name, but nobody answered. After thirty minutes of searching the entire fair, we concluded they were gone. We jogged back to the parking lot to see if they'd left as a prank, knowing they would never leave us maliciously, but Camille's car was still parked where we had left it. That's when we all started to argue.

Tony said we should stay until we find them. Marcus said no way; we have to leave. On the other hand, I proposed we find something to write on and leave a note on her windshield stating we'd left.

"Home is two fucking towns over!" Tony yelled at me. "We're not

UNEXPLAINABLE HAPPENINGS: CHILLING TRUE STORIES

walking that far. We won't make it back until tomorrow morning! And what about our friends? What if they're hurt?" he asked me. That was my initial thought, too: *what if they're hurt?* I decided to look around for them one final time, but Marcus was too scared to go back.

"I'll wait by the car," he whimpered, so Tony and I left him in the parking lot. We covered every inch of the fairground for a second time and still had no luck finding our friends. We called their names, went inside abandoned buildings, and even searched inside booths for them. No luck. Tony and I reached a point where we had to start reasoning. They weren't there, and Camille had the car keys. Our only option was to walk home. We could've called the police, but we didn't want to get any of us in trouble for trespassing, so we bit the bullet and hit the road on foot. We eventually split ways once we entered our town, individually heading to our own homes. Luckily, I made it back just before my parents woke.

I tried to call Camille the following afternoon, but she didn't answer. I also tried calling two other friends who disappeared that night, but they didn't answer either. Only Tony and Marcus showed up to school the following day, and we had to brainstorm our next move. The possibility of them getting injured, kidnapped, or, God forbid, dying was very likely to us— and we were panicking to the point of feeling sick to our stomachs.

Scared to death over our missing friends and the potential consequences, we decided to wait just one more day before notifying the police, holding on to whatever hope we had left. Luckily, the following day, Camille and our other two friends showed up to school, and by the time lunch rolled around, we had an abundance of questions to ask.

"What the hell, you guys?" Marcus yelled at them. "We were worried you got hurt, or worse, died!"

"Excuse me? You're the ones who left without saying anything. Who does that? And you didn't even bother answering our phone calls this morning!" Camille raged.

"What are you talking about? We spent hours searching the entire fairgrounds for you three, and you weren't there. Because of you, we had to walk all the way home. And none of you answered *our* phone calls, not the other way around!" Tony shouted back.

"Yeah, we were worried something terrible happened. You guys just vanished. Where'd you go?" I asked them. They exchanged glances of confusion before answering me. Camille and the two boys claimed to have been there the entire time and that we three, Tony, Marcus, and me, went missing. I then asked why they didn't come to school yesterday, and Camille's response was perhaps the most disturbing part of it all.

"What are you talking about? Yesterday is when we made the fairground plans. We were all here."

"No," I responded, "that was two days ago, Camille." She laughed at us and asked if we were on drugs, stating it was Thursday.

"It's Friday," Marcus spoke lightly, hesitantly opening his school schedule to show her. "See, they announced we'd have a school assembly this afternoon, and it's on the weekly schedule, right here, written on Friday." The three of them froze up as if they'd seen a ghost, refusing to accept they had missed an entire day's worth of time.

According to them, they were having a great time until realizing they hadn't seen Marcus, Tony, or me in a while. They then walked all over the fairgrounds in search of us until morning. Once the sun started to rise, they agreed to go home and get ready for school and that if we didn't get in touch with them by that night, they'd call the police. Similar to the plan we had. However, they thought the following morning was actually two days later. That means Camille and the boys spent two nights at the fairgrounds. How to begin explaining that, I'm unsure.

UNEXPLAINABLE HAPPENINGS: CHILLING TRUE STORIES

This story has never left our circle until now, we felt nobody would ever believe us, and it was best to keep the entire incident a secret. We have no idea what happened that night or how it could be possible. We collectively tried researching the fair's history, when and why it was abandoned, but we couldn't find any answers. Its history, name, and existence; nothing about it is accessible or searchable. The deserted park still sits there today.

UNEXPLAINABLE HAPPENINGS: CHILLING TRUE STORIES

Report #6

Five years after I moved away from home, my mother sold her house and moved to a small riverside cottage in Vermont. Following her first year living there, I finally got time off work to visit her from Florida. I'd never been to Vermont before, but it always struck me as dreamy. She'd start her mornings on the quiet river nearly

UNEXPLAINABLE HAPPENINGS: CHILLING TRUE STORIES

every day before walking her dog on a forest trail nearby. It was a slow and peaceful life, something I was looking forward to experiencing with her.

I arrived at her new home in the early afternoon. She provided a property tour before brewing tea for us to enjoy on her front porch. While filling me in on her new chapter, she spoke of something very bizarre. My mother and all her neighbors regularly see a glowing orb at night that flies and hovers low to the ground. Sometimes it's white, other times orange. "No one knows what it is, but it seems innocent," Mom chuckled.

"You know that's not normal, right?" I asked, confused by her nonchalance. She laughed again, telling me that Vermont is a world of its own. There are cursed mountains that indigenous tribes wouldn't dare step foot on. They also believed the surrounding land was doomed with bad luck wherever two rivers met, and Vermont beholds endless rivers and streams that bleed into one another.

She also told a rumor about the entirety of southern Vermont. Some settlers and natives believed a gigantic slab of black crystal lies two layers beneath the surface soil, dooming all the land in the southernmost county, the same county she resides. I asked why she chose to live in a supposed 'cursed' area, and she didn't seem to take it too seriously.

"I don't think it's cursed, but there is a lot of history in these parts, that's for sure. And when it comes to the orb, I feel like I'm living in a fantasy land. It's cool, not something many would experience in their lifetime." I suppose she had a fair point. It is fascinating if the orb seems non-threatening or ominous. Either way, the idea of its existence is incomprehensibly intriguing. I also found it strange how locally accepted and acknowledged this ball of light is, yet you never hear stories of orb sightings. It's not a common phenomenon like UFOs and Bigfoot.

"I want to see the orb," I told her.

"I wish I could show it to you, Honey. It has to show itself to you. Please spend some time outside this week when it's dark. You're bound to see it at some point before you leave."

We ate dinner outside that evening, hoping to see the orb together, and though I was trying my best to be present with Mom, I couldn't resist constantly looking over my shoulder. It never revealed itself that night, so I decided to come outside every dawn and wander the property to increase my chances.

After four consecutive nights of doing this, I gave it a rest and decided to watch a movie after supper instead. My mother took her dog, Rosco, for a walk down their dirt road as I got situated on the couch, and when she came back inside, she had news to share.

"You should've come with me! The orb was hovering in the middle of the road for about five seconds!" she exclaimed as she barged through the front door. I launched off the couch to go outside and see for myself, but she said it had already gone. "It was bright orange and hovered down the way, about as high off the ground as I am tall. Rosco and I stopped to observe, and once it finished hovering, it zipped down the road and was gone in a flash," she smiled. "It was so cool."

"At this point, I'm starting to think this whole thing is fake. How come you and your neighbors see it so often, but I haven't once in the past four nights I've been here?" I asked, doubting the existence of the orb. She shrugged and told me she didn't know what to say. So, I continued watching my show in slight bitterness, having given up on this hovering ball of light completely.

My vacation approaches its end and my final night of visiting rolls into place. Before returning to the city, I wanted to soak in every ounce of my beautiful surroundings for a last time, so I grabbed a bottle of wine and brought it down to the dock, admiring the moon-kissed river. My mother was on a work call in the cottage, so I was alone by the water. I observed the glistening waves and how they reflected the moon's glow, and as I absorbed this specific detail, the glowing grew more prominent. I thought: *Woah, you can vividly see the moon's reflection. The water is like a mirror,* only to realize it wasn't the moon's reflection I was looking at; it was the orb.

Shining like a star shedding its stunning white light, it hovered over the center of the river, subtly dancing in place. I gazed in amazement, not one bit frightened by the sighting. It was so whimsical, like I was living in a fairytale world. The orb put on a brilliant show, as if it mutually acknowledged my presence, then it zipped down the river in a flash like a shooting star burning off in the sky. I felt tempted to run inside and tell Mom about the encounter, but something held me back. "Let me just soak this in a little longer," I told myself. My mother was so happy to hear I finally saw the mysterious orb, even poking fun at me by saying: "See, I told you it was real!"

It was a beautiful moment, the orb showing itself to me in the manner it did. That evening was unforgettable, and the question remains. What exactly is this orb? Where did it come from, and why does it linger in this area? Though the idea may frighten some, I found the experience charming overall.

Thank you for reading my story; though it may not be as creepy as

UNEXPLAINABLE HAPPENINGS: CHILLING TRUE STORIES

other reports, I hope you enjoyed this unusual phenomenon. Best regards.

UNEXPLAINABLE HAPPENINGS: CHILLING TRUE STORIES

Report #7

Everybody's heard of sleep paralysis, the inability to move during the REM phase of dreaming. Many people claim they're fully conscious during their sleep paralysis experiences and that the sightings of dark entities or their inability to move were real, not a mind-trick phase between slumber and awareness. Some believe it's a spiritual or demonic force holding them down to the bed, paralyzing them while they helplessly lie awake.

Bizarre things come to me in the dream realm— if there's an unacknowledged energy in a household, I usually find out after spending a night there. I don't believe I experience sleep paralysis; it's an ability to see what's genuinely around, though commonly accepted as sleep paralysis. Google suggests what I experience is normal, but I'm here to tell you why it's not. Besides, our society likes to separate science from spirituality— convincing the public that they are total opposites. I firmly believe they are the same and that scientists could explain spiritual happenings through alternative studies if we cared to bring the two together.

Anyway, I have seen a shadow man in my dreams since I was a little girl. If you investigate it, this sighting is widespread among sleep paralysis experiences. However, I only ever see him in a home with an intense history behind it. For example, my aunt lived in a house part of the underground railroad. Her home had secret doors, hidden tunnel entrances in her basement, and you could shift sections of the ceiling to climb up into the attic. The historic society passed a law to protect these homes and preserve their significant history, so my aunt's house looked exactly how it did when its design purposes were to free and hide enslaved people.

Every night I slept there, I would see things. I would see a dark silhouette of a man standing in corners of rooms, and my little cousin would see him in broad daylight, something I've yet experienced. Almost every night I spent at my aunt's, I'd wake up in bed, paralyzed and petrified, as this thing would stalk me from across the room. While sleeping in my home, which was newer and never had a death occur inside of it, I slept like a baby, never experiencing 'sleep paralysis' once. These details were too specific to be written off as a coincidence. Why would I consistently see things in a house that was two hundred years old but nowhere else? It didn't seem as uncomplicated to say my REM sleep was playing tricks on me.

When I was eleven, I had a close friend named Annie who lived in an old Victorian house. Mind you, I'm from Massachusetts, one of the country's oldest and most historical states. It was common for people to reside in homes dating back to the early 1900s or late 1800s. Sure, people would renovate the interior for safety and style, but the foundation would remain the same. There are neighborhoods, towns even, full of historical residences. My best friend at the time lived in a traditional Victorian home built in 1910, and everything about it was authentic to its original form. Even some of their furniture belonged to the original owners.

Whenever her mom was out, and we were there alone, we'd remain glued by the hip. Scared to be alone in the house, we'd take bathroom trips together, grab food from the kitchen together, everything. We always felt that someone was watching us and would sense objects moving from the corner of our eyes. Even when we were the only ones home, it never felt that way. And we never felt entirely safe.

One night, her elderly dog peed on her bed, so we made a nest on her bedroom floor as a temporary sleeping arrangement. Hours after we'd fallen asleep, I randomly woke and sat forward. I remember mindlessly staring at Annie for a long time as she slept beside me. It felt like I had no control over my actions, but I was simultaneously aware of what I was doing. After watching Annie sleep, I steadily rose to my feet and headed out the door, which was already open, though we always fell asleep with it closed. I wasn't dreaming because I was hyper-aware, but I wasn't acting like myself. I walked down her dark hallway without a worry in the world, even though darkness was my greatest fear at the time.

I walked across her entire house until I reached a walk-in closet Annie's mom had converted into a miniature library. It was about seven feet long and five feet wide, not very spacious, and resided in a part of the house Annie and I found creepiest. I opened the closet door, shut it behind me, then sat in the fetal position facing the back corner of the wall. As the sun started to peer into the window, I woke in that position, not having moved once, and instantly freaked out. I remembered casually going into that room but was terrified to be alone; my normal, fearful self had returned. I ran into Annie's room and told her I had just woken up in the small library.

"You sleepwalked?" she shouted, startled by my story.

"No, I wasn't dreaming, I remember doing it, but I couldn't stop myself. I think I was possessed," I told Annie, goosebumps covering my body at the thought of what had happened. I also mentioned how her bedroom door was already open when I walked out, though we locked it before bed.

I later told my mother about the bizarre occurrence, but Annie didn't dare tell hers. Her mother was constantly irritated by our fear of the house. "You two are so dramatic! Do you have to go to the bathroom together?" she would say to us regularly. And though I lived in a crowded apartment with three siblings, Annie started to sleep over with me as much as her mom would

UNEXPLAINABLE HAPPENINGS: CHILLING TRUE STORIES

allow, also terrified to get possessed in her own home. The moral of the story, not all sleep paralysis is a dream, and not all sleepwalking is normal. If we combined science and spirituality into one, we could further dig into the root cause of these happenings and what makes certain people susceptible. I'm getting chills as I write this!

UNEXPLAINABLE HAPPENINGS: CHILLING TRUE STORIES

Are you enjoying the read?

I have decided to give back to the readers by making the following eBook **FREE!**

To claim your free eBook, head over to

www.LivingAmongBigfoot.com

and click the "FREE BOOK" tab!

Report #8

I'm a single mother to my daughter, Tess, who had a baby at sixteen. Yes, I'm a very young grandmother. Helping Tess with her baby has not been easy for anyone involved. She's juggling school and parenting with my physical, emotional, and financial support. Neither of us gets much sleep, as you can imagine, and funds were already

UNEXPLAINABLE HAPPENINGS: CHILLING TRUE STORIES

low before her pregnancy. When I felt life hit rock bottom, it only got worse, but in the last way that one would expect.

When my granddaughter, Molly, turned two years old, she developed impressive verbal skills. Molly knew how to say please, thank you, I'm hungry, I'm tired, and ask where we are going, can we watch a movie, how big is one hundred, etc.; she's pretty intelligent. English was the only language spoken around her, so when we heard her speaking fluent Spanish out of nowhere, there was a rise of concern. I asked my daughter how Molly speaks Spanish better than English, and my daughter didn't have the slightest clue. Molly didn't watch

Spanish shows or go to daycare yet, so we couldn't understand how she absorbed it. The strangest part of it all wasn't the Spanish itself; it was that she would only speak it to her imaginary friend, and every time she talked to her imaginary friend, she would look up at the ceiling. It was very uncomfortable for my daughter and me to watch.

One night, while my daughter and I were cooking dinner together, we realized Molly was no longer in the kitchen. We last saw her at the kitchen table drawing; surely, we would've heard her struggle to get down from her chair and leave the room. After looking all over the house for her, we started to panic. How was

UNEXPLAINABLE HAPPENINGS: CHILLING TRUE STORIES

this possible? How could this toddler disappear from the home? Before calling the police, my daughter checked the lower kitchen cabinets, the only area left unsearched.

"There's no way she's in a cabinet," I said, holding my phone and ready to call 911. To my surprise, I was wrong. Our cabinets didn't have dividing walls between them; if you opened one of them and poked your head in, you could see behind every other cabinet door, like a small hallway. Molly was sitting in the cabinets, giggling and whispering Spanish to her imaginary friend.

We couldn't hear her quiet voice while cooking because we also had the radio playing, but when we looked inside to see what she was doing, it was like she was in a trance, unable to hear or see us next to her. Suddenly, Molly looked around the cabinet area in confusion and asked her imaginary friend a question in English: "Where are you?"

"Where's who, Molly?" Tess asked her daughter.

"My friend!" she pouted.

"What does your friend look like?" I asked.

"Tall! He's very tall," she responded, sending shivers through our veins. After that, there was a week of calmness. Molly stopped talking to her imaginary friend as if he had left and never returned. But once that peaceful week ended, a new level of fuckery arrived. And it was far more worrying than my granddaughter suddenly speaking fluent Spanish.

I watched a movie in the living room while the girls slept upstairs in their shared bedroom. I heard a muffled sound echoing above me but decided to ignore it. Then, I realized what it was. My daughter was in the stairway crying.

"Tess, are you okay?" I asked her after pausing my movie. The weeping continued, so I asked again. There was still no response, and her crying grew more intense. I then began to walk up the stairway to console her, but once I reached the turning point and could see the top

UNEXPLAINABLE HAPPENINGS: CHILLING TRUE STORIES

half of the staircase, the crying simultaneously stopped as I noticed she was no longer there. Before looking up the stairs, I could've sworn she was right there. Her cries sounded so close. Confused, I walked to their bedroom and cracked open the door. She was lying in bed with Molly, both seemingly asleep.

"Tess?" I whispered.

"Hm?" she moaned.

"Were you just crying on the staircase?" I asked her.

"Mom, no, I'm sleeping," she said grumpily. And that confirmed it; I just heard what sounded exactly like my daughter crying on the stairs, her sobs echoing across the house clear as day, except she was sleeping the entire time. The following morning I told her what had happened over breakfast. She was alarmed, to say the least, and said she thought she heard me crying later that night after I checked on her, but she heard it coming from the living room. After seeing I wasn't downstairs, she got scared and ran back into her bedroom. Something was playing mind tricks on us, convincing us that the other was crying.

About four days later, we three girls watched a movie together after dinner. During this time, somebody started aggressively knocking on our front door. I asked my daughter if she was expecting anyone, to which she shook her head no, so I got up to see who was eagerly trying to reach us. Nobody was there. I figured it was neighborhood kids pranking us, so I locked the door and began walking back to the living room as if nothing had happened. The loud knocking returned as I passed the basement, but it wasn't coming from the front door anymore.

Stunned by what I thought was happening, I slowly turned around to look at the basement door. It shook with every hard knock as I stood before it. I stared at it for a moment, paralyzed by fear, until my survival instincts kicked in. I ran to the living room and demanded that the girls get up. Without questioning, Tess threw

Bella over her shoulder, and we ran out the door in our socks. We spent that night at my brother's house a town over while I had police search our home for the intruder. There were no signs of anyone being in my house besides us girls.

We stayed in that house for an additional two months before biting the bullet and moving out. During those last two months, my daughter and I continued to hear one another speaking, similar to the staircase incident. I heard Tess yell out for my help when she wasn't home, and she heard me call her name from the basement while I was at work. Sleeping at night became difficult, and we all slept in the same room during those final months. By sleeping together, we could easily determine whether the voices we heard were authentic. Except we never heard them while we were together, only when we were alone and vulnerable.

I'm happy to say those imitations of our voices went away after we moved out. Part of me wants to believe that the house *is* haunted, but there was never any weird activity throughout the many years we lived there until Molly became a toddler. Was an ill-intended spirit passing through? Did something latch on to either of us three girls and follow us home? I'm clueless about it all because I've never believed in ghosts or paranormal activity, so the strange

UNEXPLAINABLE HAPPENINGS: CHILLING TRUE STORIES

happenings we endured are challenging for me to wrap my brain around.

Thank you for reading my story. I hope this makes it into your remarkable series. If you find it fitting, I'm eager to see what the public says about it. May God be with you all.

Report #9

Throughout my entire life, I've never known what it feels like to be lonely. I have an identical twin brother, Jason, and he and I have been best friends since birth. We played the same sports, shared the same humor, and even had the same friends. Believe it or not, I can't recall ever arguing with him. Jason and I were close for the first thirty years of our lives, so when he went missing, you could imagine the pain it brought upon my life.

It was the week of our thirtieth birthday; Jason drove to visit where I lived in New Mexico, not a far trek from where we grew up in Arizona, but I was new to the state, and he had yet seen my place. He spent a week with me at my house, and we devoted our time to doing tourist things, like exploring Santa Fe, stargazing in the desert, and hitting the state's most popular hikes. He told me that, alongside Arizona, New Mexico has the most UFO sightings and unexplainable disappearances. We were both really into extraterrestrial theories, so I didn't think anything of it at the time. It was usual for us to discuss such things.

With that being said, ever since the day Jason disappeared, I can't help but compare his tragedy to alleged alien abductions. He quite literally vanished, almost right in front of my eyes. I can't blame myself for the incident, but I wish I had kept my eyes on him. If I hadn't looked away, I would at least know what had happened. The 'what-ifs' have been destroying me, though I suppose it's a natural part of the grieving process.

His disappearance took place on the last night of his stay. We were smoking a cigarette on my porch when he decided to show me the stunts his new car does when he locks and unlocks it. I remained seated by my front door while Jason crossed the parking lot. He wasn't far, maybe twenty-five feet from where I sat. He clicked the unlock button and laughed like a little kid as his side mirrors extended, then locked it back up to show me how they inverted. I briefly turned my attention to the table beside me so I could set my drink down and playfully clap for his car's performance, and as I looked back in his direction, he was gone—both him and his car.

No noise indicated he had driven away, and even if there was, it wasn't physically possible for him and his vehicle to vanish within the two seconds it took me to set my drink down. I couldn't believe my eyes. They were gone, and I refused to accept it as possible; even convincing myself at one point that I was dreaming and slapping myself to try and wake from the dreadful nightmare. But I never woke up, and Jason hasn't reappeared since. We went on the missing person's list with posters hung all over the surrounding area and in our hometown. Jason's car information was provided on the signs too, but there's been no luck finding either, and it's been six years since the incident.

Can you think of any logical explanation for what may've happened? You can't. My family thinks I'm crazy for even considering an alien abduction, nor do they believe he disappeared in thin air as I say he did. I'm at a significant loss and pray that wherever Jason is if he's alive, he is not suffering. Next month we'd be turning thirty-six together.

Report #10

Hello, I'm Eva, a small-town girl from rural Maine, and I have a very odd story regarding an unexplainable happening I experienced four years back. My then-boyfriend and I were driving to his house after a dinner date and decided to take a long way home, also known as the backroads. Backroads in our area guide you on a beautiful journey through the woods, and we loved cruising by while listening to our music. More often than not, we'd go driving on the backroads just for the hell of it when we had nothing else to do. It's a small-town thing.

So, that's what we were doing; windows down, music blasting, like every other night, until we drove past something we found to be a bit strange. A man was on the side of the road facing a tree with his back turned to us. He stood completely still like a mannequin; his face was so close to the tree that we couldn't see it as we passed. He was wearing gloves and a long winter coat though it was summer. "What the hell, did you see that guy facing the tree like that?" I asked my boyfriend, unsure of what was going on.

"Yeah, that was weird," he laughed, "should we turn around and see if he's still doing it?" he asked playfully. We had nowhere to be, so I said yes, and he pulled a u-turn in the middle of the road. We drove past where the man had stood, but he was no longer there.

"He's not there!" I said in shock, for not even two minutes had passed since we last saw him. "Did we just see a ghost?" I asked, slightly frightened. No houses were nearby, and it was extremely dark outside since there weren't streetlights or moonlight due to the heavy clouds. If it weren't for our car's headlights, we wouldn't have been able to see him at all. To think that this man was alone

UNEXPLAINABLE HAPPENINGS: CHILLING TRUE STORIES

in the pitch dark and staring at a tree before vanishing was very unsettling. We pulled another U-turn to direct ourselves home again, and the man reappeared a quarter mile down the road from where we initially saw him, and once again, his back was facing us, but he was now staring off into the woods rather than facing a tree.

"How is that possible?" my boyfriend gasped. "There's no way he could've made it this far so quickly, especially without us seeing him." We both looked at each other with concern, unsure of what our curiosity was getting us into. "I'm turning around again," he said before whipping his car back around. We drove slowly, both looking out the

84

UNEXPLAINABLE HAPPENINGS: CHILLING TRUE STORIES

windows to see where this man had gone next. We found him directly across the street from the first sighting. He was standing in the middle of a pullover nook, holding his body incredibly still, facing the dark forest before him. Nobody can continuously reappear on different parts of the road the way he did. It isn't possible unless you have the power of teleportation. My boyfriend stopped the car for a second to observe him, and as we watched this stranger stand entirely motionless in the dark, my intuition was screaming at me to get out of there immediately.

"Let's go, let's go now!" I squealed. "Please, go!" I then yelled at him. We sped off to be away from the

UNEXPLAINABLE HAPPENINGS: CHILLING TRUE STORIES

man but unfortunately had to make a fourth U-turn to head back in the direction of home. I was terrified to the point of nausea by the idea of passing this person again, scared to see where they'd be standing next, what they'd be staring at, and if they'd turn their attention to us. He didn't reappear on our fourth drive-by. We both kept an eye out, but he was out of sight. What was once an ordinary evening turned into a horror story, and we were incomprehensibly stunned by it all. Unsure of what was truly happening with that man, I saged my boyfriend's entire house when we arrived as he locked every door. Not that we thought this man would come to the house; he had no idea where we lived, but then again,

UNEXPLAINABLE HAPPENINGS: CHILLING TRUE STORIES

who knows what's probable. I randomly think of it to this day, especially when I'm driving down that same road. I can't conjure a solid explanation for it— it was simply unexplainable.

Report #11

Dear Autumn and Tom, I hope this email finds you well. I'm reaching out to share an unexplainable occurrence that I experienced this year, hoping that you'll find it useful for your new series. It's relatively short, yet I thought you two might be interested.

My close friend Stephan moved into a new house and wanted me to see it, so he invited me for a couple of beers after work. As I was on my way,

UNEXPLAINABLE HAPPENINGS: CHILLING TRUE STORIES

he called and said he was being held up at the office and would be running late, telling me to welcome myself inside while I waited.

I found his spare key under the doormat and invited myself in. Immediately, a large black cat ran to greet me at the door. I didn't know he had a cat, so I assumed he adopted it after moving in. I hung out with this cat for an hour while waiting for Stephan to arrive. Before resting on the kitchen window sill, he cuddled beside me for a good while. Eventually, the cat begged at the back door for me to let him outside. I noticed Stephan's backyard was fenced in, so I assumed it'd be okay to let the cat roam.

About ten minutes later, the cat was meowing to get let in. I opened the door, and a white cat strutted inside. I was surprised by this. Initially unaware Stephan even had cats, I tried to call him and ask if the white one was his too. He didn't answer. The white cat seemed comfortable in Stephan's home, so I figured it must be his. Then the white cat meowed to go outside, so I let him. Soon after doing this, Stephan walked through the front door. I greeted him and offered him one of the beers I had brought, and we sat on his couch to catch up with one another.

"I didn't know you were a cat guy," I said to him.

"I'm not," he grunted.

"Then why'd you get two of them?" I laughed. He faced me with a look of surprise.

"You see them too?" he asked in astonishment. I was very confused by his question at first, asking him what he meant by that.

"I don't have cats," he said, "the black one appeared in my home out of nowhere last week and approached me. I asked a girl I had over if she had let him inside, and she didn't know what I was talking about. The cat was sitting at my feet, clear as day, and I asked her, 'do you not see this cat?'" My heart began to sink as I realized where this story was heading. "She told me there was no cat and asked if I was okay. You could tell she was worried. So, I took a picture of it on my phone, and as I clicked on the image afterward, there was no cat, just my feet resting on the floor. I thought I was losing my mind. You have no idea how relieved I am that you saw it too."

"What the fuck?" I yelled, unable to believe what I was hearing. "Have you seen the white one too?" I asked him. Stephan said he'd only seen the white cat once but sees the black cat nearly every day. He genuinely started to believe he was losing his mind, but I confirmed that wasn't the case. Stephan told me it would constantly appear in his house without being let inside. He'd randomly spot the cat sitting on his bed, strutting on the kitchen counters, lying on the couch, or simply passing by and brushing against his leg.

I'm sure you've heard of ghost sightings, but have you heard about phantom animals? Pretty funny in a peculiar way.

Report #12

Fair warning: this report is graphic and may upset those grieving the loss of a loved one.

In 2016, my mom informed me that my uncle had called and was feeling very sick, so she asked me to bring him over some soup she had made. When I arrived at his house, it was dark outside, so I wasn't very mindful of my surroundings. I knocked on his door several times before attempting to allow myself in, thinking he was too sick to get up. He locked his door, so I struck again and again until I heard a loud thud and cracking noise behind me.

I twirled and saw my uncle's body lying on the pavement behind me. Forensic pathologists later concluded through investigation that he had jumped off his roof and plummeted to his death, ruling it a suicide. Of course, my family and I had a challenging time coming to terms with this. And the memory of his lifeless body haunted me, keeping me awake for days.

My uncle seemed more excited about life than anyone I knew. He was a world traveler, having just arrived home after spending two months in Peru when I tried to bring him my mother's soup. While in Peru, he mentioned how much he loved that country and told our family where he planned to fly next. He had so many plans and enthusiasm; ending his own life on a whim was impossible for us to accept.

One month later, our family got together to celebrate the memory of his life and bury him beside my great-grandmother. Lowering his casket into the ground is when it finally hit me; he was gone. My uncle owned his house, so there was no authoritative pressure for us to empty his belongings by any deadline. Friends and family eventually gathered in his

UNEXPLAINABLE HAPPENINGS: CHILLING TRUE STORIES

home to try and manage his possessions. As I was helping to carry his couch down the stairs and move it into a U-Haul truck, I heard my uncle's voice call out, "what are you doing?" agitatedly. I dropped my end of the couch in shock and looked over to my cousin, who was lugging it with me. "I just heard Uncle Ray's voice," I gasped, tears coming to my eyes.

"I heard that too," my cousin replied, just as shaken as I.

"Hey! Stop!" his voice yelled, echoing from down the hallway.

"Ray?" my aunt shrieked. My cousin and I exchanged looks of skepticism. Did everyone hear his voice? Ray stormed around the corner and approached us.

"What are you doing?" he shouted again. Everyone looked like they'd seen a ghost because, deep down, we all thought it was his ghost. "Is nobody going to answer me? What the fuck!" he threw his duffle bag to the ground before demanding we return all his belongings to their places.

"Ray, is that you?" I cried.

"No shit! Somebody, please tell me what's happening!" he said, his face red with anger.

"This isn't possible," my aunt wailed, "you died!"

"Died? I was in Peru. Everybody knows that."

"No, Ray, you died!" my aunt screamed, dropping to the floor. Auntie was convinced we were interacting with his wandering spirit, but I was starting to realize that wasn't the case. My uncle was standing before me, alive and well. I ran up and hugged him tighter than ever before, allowing my tears to pour onto his shirt as I embraced his warm body and strong heartbeat beneath his chest.

While holding him, my mind convinced me that I was dreaming, as I'm sure others were convinced of the same, but it was only a matter of time before we collectively accepted the truth. We weren't dreaming. Uncle Ray is here. I told Ray I had seen him jump off his roof and kill himself a month prior and that we had already buried his body and held a service for him. When I tell you I've never seen another human look so terrified, I mean it. Uncle Ray's face turned pale as he told me, "That's impossible. I just arrived from Peru." My mother then turned to me, questioning whether I was sure it was him who fell off the roof.

I doubted myself for a moment before remembering what I had seen. And what I saw was Ray. It was undoubtedly him. I saw his face turned to the side as he lay lifeless on the pavement. I also mentioned that my mother said he called her right

UNEXPLAINABLE HAPPENINGS: CHILLING TRUE STORIES

before the death occurred, claiming that he was home and feeling unwell.

"I never called you and said that," he said, accusatorially staring at my mother.

"Yes, you did. I almost didn't answer the call because it was coming from an unknown number, but it was you. Your voice, your mannerisms, Ray, you told me you were home!" she said defensively.

"Wait, why didn't we hear from you for the entire month we thought you were dead?" my cousin finally asked him. We all turned to Ray, waiting for a good explanation.

"My phone broke, and I didn't want to get a new one while I was there, then I'd have a Peruvian area code," he told us. "I emailed you explaining that I'll be out of touch. I asked you to pass the message along," he snarked at my aunt. She pulled out her phone and went through her email inbox, denying that she had ever received such a message. However, it was there. Deep in her email was a statement from Ray that dated one day before his supposed death, clarifying why he'll be out of touch.

Authorities dug up the body buried under Ray's tombstone for examination. If Ray is alive, we need to know for whom we held a service. The craziest part is that the man was deemed unidentifiable. There were no records of him to be found. It's as if

UNEXPLAINABLE HAPPENINGS: CHILLING TRUE STORIES

this doppelganger teleported to Ray's roof from another dimension and jumped off. Nobody could make sense of it, not even the detectives. It remains a burdening mystery, but we're thankful to have Uncle Ray back.

Report #13

My name is David, and I'm a senior park ranger who recently retired after dedicating twenty years of service to one of the most beautiful pieces of land. It was the perfect job for me, hence why I stayed so long, and most days on the clock felt like a walk in the park, no pun intended. However, during my second to last year working at the park, I experienced what I believe was a ghost leading me to his body.

UNEXPLAINABLE HAPPENINGS: CHILLING TRUE STORIES

I was driving around on a work ATV as dusk was approaching, ensuring tourists and hikers knew that the park was closing soon and informing any campers that it was time to return to their designated campsite. While doing this, I noticed some belongings left behind in the forest off-trail. I drove the ATV into the woods, following the discarded items tossed like litter and collecting them. I picked up a sleeping bag, a wool hat, a book, and stuff of that sort, all of which were molded and seemingly left behind years ago. I thought it was strange no one had come and collected these trashed items sooner, then remembered how vast the park was. It would be easy to miss something like this.

Once I managed the mess and was ready to return to the trail, the ATV wouldn't start. It had died entirely, which surprised me since it was less than a year old. I called for someone to pick me up, and my colleagues said it would be an hour until they could reach me since I was far away from the main cabin. I decided to make myself comfortable and leaned against a nearby oak. That's when I heard the voices shouting in the distance.

It sounded like two men arguing, except one was extremely angry while the other communicated timidly. Amid the muffled sounds, a few things said came across clear as day. "It wasn't yours to take!" and

"Fuck you, it was mine!" indicated that the argument had reached a boiling point between the two. I called out and asked if they were all right, but I didn't get a response. That one voice kept yelling at the other with increasing anger.

Though I didn't think it was feasible, the yelling grew louder and more intense than before. I started to walk in their direction to try and ease the tension for safety and courtesy purposes, but as I took my first few steps, a gunshot fired. Then everything went silent. I immediately returned to the ATV and hid behind it, calling my colleagues and informing them about the potential danger. The other rangers didn't arrive until dark, and though we tried searching for the two men, we were out of luck. I returned to that area the next day to speculate in the sunlight; that's when I found the body.

I scanned what I assumed was the place they were arguing at, the rocky terrain corner of the forest. Nobody usually wanders in this area, for it's not easy to walk on, and there aren't any long-distance views like there are in the rest of the park, but I was confident that area is where their voices traveled from. As I was starting to feel unlucky with my search, I stumbled across a bullet shell. It was too old to have been from what I had heard the previous day. However, hunting is prohibited at the park, so

UNEXPLAINABLE HAPPENINGS: CHILLING TRUE STORIES

there shouldn't have been a bullet shell on the property. It encouraged me to search more extensively.

About twenty feet from the bullet was a white object revealing itself from a crevasse between two large rocks. It was thin, lanky, and sharp-looking. Having never seen anything like that before, I approached it. The closer I got, the more I realized the park I've been patrolling for so long isn't exactly what I thought it to be— it holds dark secrets. The white object was a skeletal foot. I shined a light into the dark crevasse and found the rest of the body. The skeleton was wrapped in old, moldy, matted men's clothing. But

UNEXPLAINABLE HAPPENINGS: CHILLING TRUE STORIES

that one foot that caught my attention was missing a boot.

The autopsy reports declared that this man died from a gunshot wound to the skull. They estimated his date of death to be forty years before I found the remains. The park was then closed to the public for a widespread investigation around the land. We didn't find any additional human remains or evidence of other deaths, which leads me to believe the skeleton I saw belonged to one of the men I heard arguing. It's the only explanation I can think of.

Conclusion

Thanks for reading! If you're looking for more, be sure to read *Unexplainable Happenings: Chilling True Stories, Volume 2.*

UNEXPLAINABLE HAPPENINGS: CHILLING TRUE STORIES

Editor's Note

Before you go, I'd like to say "thank you" for purchasing this book.

I know you had various cryptid-related books to choose from, but you took a chance with my content.
Therefore, thanks for reading this one and sticking with it to the last page.

At this point, I'd like to ask you for a *tiny* favor; it would mean the world to me if you could leave a review wherever you purchased this book.

Your feedback will aid me as I continue to create products that you and many others can enjoy.

UNEXPLAINABLE HAPPENINGS: CHILLING TRUE STORIES

UNEXPLAINABLE HAPPENINGS: CHILLING TRUE STORIES

Mailing List Sign-Up Form

Don't forget to sign up for the newsletter email list. I promise I will not use it to spam you but to ensure that you always receive the first word on any new releases, discounts, or giveaways! All you need to do is visit the following URL and enter your email address.

URL-

http://eepurl.com/dhnspT

UNEXPLAINABLE HAPPENINGS: CHILLING TRUE STORIES

Social Media

Feel free to follow/reach out to me with questions or concerns on either Instagram or Twitter! I will do my best to follow back and respond to all comments.

Instagram:

@living_among_bigfoot

Twitter:

@AmongBigfoot

UNEXPLAINABLE HAPPENINGS: CHILLING TRUE STORIES

About the Author

Since a young age, Autumn Barnes has endured involuntary contact with the spiritual realm, seeing things many others don't. Recently, she's felt inspired to share her shocking experiences with the world, hoping to bring more attention to this disturbing yet very real phenomenon.

Printed in Great Britain
by Amazon